FOREWORD

Starting at a mere 99p, my ebooks are
intentionally priced to be accessible to everyone.
I believe that wisdom and inspiration should be within reach of all,
regardless of budget constraints. By keeping the prices low, I aim to
ensure that individuals and
families can embark on a transformative journey without worrying
about their wallets.

Doing My Bit: I firmly believe in the power of collective support
and helping one another. By setting my ebook prices at the minimum
allowed by Amazon, I hope to contribute my small part in enabling
people to access these valuable resources, ensuring that financial
limitations never hinder personal growth and
development. Together, we can build a community that shares
knowledge, uplifts one another, and thrives!

Join the affordable wisdom revolution today! Head to Amazon and
grab a copy of my ebooks, priced at just 99p. Let's embark on a
journey of learning, growth, and financial empowerment, because
everyone deserves the chance to thrive!

MASTERING HOUSEHOLD BILLS AND FINANCES

A Guide to Saving on Bills and Navigating Food Assistance

By A. Iqbal

CHAPTER 1:

Introduction

As families face increasing costs of living, it is important to understand the underlying factors contributing to rising household bills.

One such factor is the rising cost of energy due to the unpredictable fluctuations in the market. Additionally, the cost of food has also been increasing steadily, making it harder for families to maintain a balanced budget.

Another key contributor to rising household bills is the debt load carried by many families. With high-interest rates, it can be difficult to make progress towards paying down debts, and this can lead to a cycle of ongoing financial stress.

Families must also contend with discretionary and non-discretionary spending which can quickly add up, leaving little room for savings. Understanding these factors is essential to establishing a solid financial foundation and achieving long-term financial stability.

In this book, we will explore how families can take action to manage their household bills effectively. Through practical strategies, we can help ease the burden of rising costs and build a better financial future for ourselves and our loved ones.

Have you ever opened your mail to find your bills piling up?

Have you ever felt overwhelmed and helpless while trying to manage your household expenses?

You are not alone. Many families are struggling to keep up with the rising cost of living, and the lack of financial literacy only makes things worse. But there is a solution.

The urgency for managing household bills cannot be emphasised enough. The consequences of neglecting your finances can be devastating, leading to debt, bankruptcy, and even homelessness. Therefore, it is crucial to take action now and learn how to manage your expenses effectively. In this book, you will find practical and proven strategies that will help you cut down your costs, increase your income, and save for your future. You will learn how to assess your current situation, identify opportunities for improvement, and set realistic goals that align with your values and priorities. You will also discover how to monitor your progress, overcome obstacles, and make smart adjustments along the way. By applying the principles in this book, you will not only achieve your financial goals but also enhance your quality of life.

You will have more peace of mind, more time for what matters, and more resources to create unforgettable memories with your loved ones. So, let's get started. The journey towards financial freedom and abundance awaits you.

Households all over the world are facing a constant challenge of rising household bills. The cost of living is only increasing, and it is up to each and every one of us to manage these household bills effectively.
I understand how daunting it can be to stay on top of every bill and payment, but there are numerous advantages to doing so.
Firstly, managing your household bills effectively means that you have a clearer understanding of your financial situation. This enables you to make proactive decisions to adjust your spending and saving habits accordingly. By having a clear picture of your expenses and income, it is easier to set realistic financial goals and achieve them. Additionally, managing your bills can lead to significant savings over time. Just a few simple changes in your daily habits such as using energy-efficient appliances or minimising water usage, and smart shopping for groceries can free up a significant amount of money that can be directed towards your savings or investment plan.

Moreover, knowing exactly where your money is going can bring peace of mind and eliminate stress around paying bills. You will no longer have to worry about missing payments, incurring late fees or interest, or hurting your credit score. This sense of financial security allows you to focus on other important areas of your life, such as your family, career, and personal growth.

To achieve these benefits, it is essential to set realistic goals and establish a strategy to manage your household bills more effectively.

This book is designed to guide you through the process of assessing your current situation, identifying cost-cutting strategies, boosting your income, saving more money, and monitoring your progress. By following the practical tips and advice in this book, you can achieve financial stability and peace of mind for you and your family.

In order for families to effectively manage their household bills during times of rising costs of living, it is crucial to establish specific, measurable, achievable, realistic, and time-bound goals. Without clear goals, it can be easy to become overwhelmed or not know where to start.

Setting goals that are specific means that they are clear and precise. For example, setting a goal to "reduce energy costs" is not specific enough. Instead, a specific goal might be to "reduce energy costs by 15% over the next 6 months". This allows for clear understanding of what needs to be achieved and how progress will be measured. Measurable goals are important because they allow for tracking of progress and accountability. This means setting goals that have a number attached to them, whether that be a dollar amount or percentage reduction.

Achievable goals are those that are challenging, yet still possible to reach.

When setting goals, it is important to consider any potential roadblocks or limitations that may prevent achievement. These goals should strike a balance between being challenging yet realistic. Realistic goals are those that are feasible within the current circumstances. It is important to consider all factors and limitations when setting these goals, such as income, time, and resources.

Finally, time-bound goals have a defined timeline for completion. This creates a sense of urgency and accountability to ensure that progress is being made.

By establishing clear and specific goals that are measurable, achievable, realistic, and time-bound, families can effectively manage their household bills during times of rising costs of living. These goals provide a roadmap for success and direction for action towards a more financially stable future.

In today's world, it seems that managing household bills has become more challenging than ever before.

With the cost of living on the rise, families and households are finding it difficult to keep up with various bills that keep coming their way. But fear not, for there is a solution to this problem.

Through the contents, structure and techniques that we will cover in each chapter of the book, readers will learn how to set specific, measurable, achievable, realistic, and time-bound goals, identify unnecessary expenses, and adapt their plan based on changing circumstances and priorities. Furthermore, readers will learn how to create an emergency fund and how to save for specific financial goals, such as a child's education or retirement.

Moreover, we will discuss the benefits of cost management, such as greater financial freedom, and how it can transform your financial stability, overall health, and happiness.

CHAPTER 2:

Assessing Your Current Situation

One crucial step to managing your household bills effectively is to conduct a thorough household audit. This involves reviewing your bills, payments, and receipts to identify patterns and opportunities that can help you make informed cost-cutting decisions.

By conducting a household audit, you can gain valuable insights into how your money is being spent and identify areas where you may be overspending. For example, you may find that you're paying for subscriptions or memberships that you no longer use, or that you're spending more on eating out than you thought.

In addition to identifying areas for cost-cutting, a household audit can also help you develop good financial habits, such as keeping track of your expenses and staying on top of your bills. By reviewing your payments and receipts, you can ensure that you're not missing any payments or letting bills go unpaid.

Overall, conducting a household audit is an essential part of assessing your current financial situation and developing a baseline for improvement. It allows you to take control of your finances and make informed decisions that will help you save money and achieve your financial goals.

As families navigate through the ever-changing landscape of the cost of living, it is crucial to evaluate their current financial situation and develop a solid baseline for improvement. One of the critical steps in this process is determining the proportion of income that goes towards various household bills.

To begin, conducting a household audit is essential. Look through bills, payments, and receipts to identify patterns and opportunities with expenses. Then, calculate the bills-to-income ratio, which will determine the percentage of income that goes towards each bill. It's crucial to look at the ratio in detail, understanding which bills take up a larger portion of your monthly income.

After calculating the bills-to-income ratio, identifying your debt load is the next step. Understanding your debt balance, interest rates, and payment schedules is critical when making decisions towards your financial goals. Monitoring your debt and identifying ways to reduce it can help, as it has a direct impact on your financial health in the long run.

Thirdly, analysing spending habits is important for your family to know where the money goes each month. Categorising discretionary and non-discretionary expenses allows for easier evaluation of where improvements can be made.
Establishing priorities and values can reflect your aspirations and motivate a change in spending habits.

In conclusion, evaluating household bills' proportion against your income is an essential part of assessing your financial health. Beginning with a household audit, calculating the bills-to-income ratio and debt load, and analysing expenses gives a starting point to making informed decisions towards the family's financial goals.

As a family, it's always crucial to know where you stand financially. It's hard to know where you are going if you don't know where you're coming from, and this is especially true when it comes to your income and expenses. It's vital that you assess your current situation to gain a clear understanding of your financial baseline and make a plan for improvement.

One of the most crucial aspects of this assessment is estimating your debt balance, interest rates, and payment schedule. This is because debt can be a significant hindrance to one's financial growth. Before striving to create wealth, you must first tackle your debt. It's hard to invest, save for the future, or make any significant financial decisions when you have large obligations you cannot meet.

To estimate your debt balance, dig deep and find all the relevant documents. This could be credit card statements, loan agreements, and other financial obligation documents. Once you've assembled an accurate picture of how much you owe, you can move on to examining the interest rates and payment schedules. This step is crucial because it will help you determine how much money you need to allocate to repay your loans and how long it may take to become debt-free.

By assessing your current situation, including your debts and obligations, you can develop a baseline that will allow you to make a plan for long-term financial success. It might not be easy, but it's a significant step that will help you achieve your financial goals. Remember, it's never too late to start managing your finances better. Take charge of your financial situation, create a plan, and work towards achieving a debt-free future.

Everyone spends money in one way or another. Some expenses we consider necessary, such as bills, rent, and food, while others fall under the category of discretionary spending- the types of expenses that are considered non-essential, such as dining out or buying new clothes.

Discretionary spending can seem harmless at first, but even these small expenses can add up over time, impacting our ability to save money and achieve financial goals. This is why evaluating discretionary and non-discretionary spending is an essential part of assessing your current financial situation.

The first step in evaluating your spending is to categorise your expenses into discretionary and non-discretionary categories. Non-discretionary expenses are things that must be paid, such as rent or utilities. Discretionary expenses are things that can be reduced or eliminated without impacting your quality of life.

Once you have categorised your expenses, it's time to analyse your discretionary spending to identify areas where you can cut back. One way to do this is by making a list of all discretionary expenses for the past month. This list should include everything from coffee runs to subscriptions.

Next, review your list and see which expenses you can eliminate or reduce. This could mean canceling a subscription you don't use or cutting back on your morning coffee runs. These small steps could lead to significant financial savings over time.

Another way to reduce discretionary spending is by identifying areas where you can optimise costs. For example, instead of buying new clothes every season, consider purchasing pre-owned items from second-hand stores or online marketplaces. You can also save money by comparing prices and finding deals for things like groceries and household items.

By evaluating your discretionary and non-discretionary spending habits, you can develop a realistic baseline for improvement. This knowledge will allow you to take the necessary steps to reduce expenses, optimise costs, and allocate funds towards achieving your financial goals. Remember, every dollar counts, and by being mindful of your spending habits, you can achieve financial stability and success.

Reflecting on Your Personal Values and Goals

One of the most important steps in assessing your current financial situation is reflecting on your personal values and goals. By doing so, you can align your financial decisions with your aspirations and ensure that you're creating a financial plan that works for you.

To start, take some time to think about what's important to you. Are you passionate about travel? Do you value education for yourself or your children? Is giving back to your community a priority? These values will serve as the foundation for your financial goals.

Once you've identified your values, it's time to set specific, measurable, achievable, realistic, and time-bound (SMART) goals. For example, if travel is important to you, your goal could be to save enough money to take an annual vacation with your family. Or, if education is a priority, your goal could be to save for your child's college tuition.

When setting your goals, consider your current financial situation. How much debt do you have? What is your current income? You'll need to set goals that are achievable within your means.

It's also important to reassess your goals regularly. As your financial situation changes, your priorities may shift. For example, if you receive a raise, you may be able to increase your savings or adjust your goals to focus on a different priority.

By reflecting on your personal values and goals, you can create a financial plan that works for you. With SMART goals in place and a clear idea of what's important to you, you'll be well on your way to achieving financial success.

CHAPTER 3:

Cost-Cutting Strategies

In today's world, where expenses are skyrocketing, saving money by adopting a cost-cutting strategy has become a necessity for families and households. One of the easiest ways to do so is by adopting habits and technologies that can save money on your electricity, gas, and water bills.

Reducing your energy consumption not only helps you save money but also contributes to the environment by reducing your carbon footprint. You can achieve this by adopting simple habits such as turning off lights and electronics when not in use, using energy-efficient appliances, and making sure to unplug devices that are not in use.

Another way to save money on energy bills is by making some changes in your home that can improve its energy efficiency. Simple things like sealing air leaks, insulating your home, and using a programmable thermostat can lower your energy costs significantly.

Furthermore, making small changes to your daily routine can also go a long way in reducing your water bills. You can save water by fixing leaky taps, using low-flow shower heads, and only using the dishwasher and washing machine when they are full.

Negotiating deals with your service providers is also crucial in saving money on your bills. Many companies offer discounts if you sign up for auto-pay or paperless billing. You can also ask for a loyalty discount if you have been a customer for a long time.
In conclusion, adopting simple habits and technologies that can save money on your electricity, gas, and water bills is an effective way to cut your expenses and manage your household bills effectively. By doing so, not only will you save money but also contribute towards a better tomorrow for the environment.

In order to manage household bills during cost of living rises, one of the most effective strategies to adopt is reducing grocery and dining expenses through smart shopping, cooking, and storing tips. The average household spends a significant portion of their budget on food, and this can quickly add up. However, by being mindful and strategic with our food choices and habits, we can save a considerable amount of money without sacrificing quality or variety.

One tip is to plan meals in advance and make a grocery list before heading to the store. This can help avoid impulse buys and ensure that we only purchase what we need. Shopping in bulk for non-perishable items can also be a great way to save money in the long run.

Additionally, cooking at home instead of eating out can significantly cut down on expenses. By preparing meals in advance and utilising leftovers, families can save on both time and money. Investing in quality kitchen equipment, such as a slow cooker or pressure cooker, can also make meal preparation more efficient and cost-effective. Finally, storing food properly can help extend its lifespan and prevent unnecessary waste. This means using airtight containers, storing perishable items in the refrigerator or freezer, and keeping an eye on expiration dates.

By incorporating these cost-cutting strategies into our daily routines, families can reduce their food expenses and contribute to overall financial health and stability.

As families and households face the daunting task of managing rising bills, it is crucial to find ways to reduce expenses without compromising the quality of life. One area where significant savings can be made is by cutting down transportation costs. This includes finding ways to reduce your fuel, maintenance, and insurance expenses for your vehicles.

To start with, it is essential to keep your vehicle in good condition. Regular maintenance and servicing will not only ensure your car lasts longer but also save you money on repairs in the long run.

Simple things like keeping your tires inflated to the correct pressure and changing your air filter can improve your car's fuel efficiency and save you money on fuel.

Another way to save on transportation costs is by reducing the number of miles you drive. This can be achieved by carpooling or using public transport whenever possible. If you live in an area with good public transport links, consider selling your car and relying solely on buses, trains, or trams (if available in you area). This could save you significant amounts of money on fuel, insurance, and parking expenses.

Insurance is another significant expense for car owners. By shopping around and comparing quotes, you could save a significant amount of money on your car insurance each year.

When it comes to fuel costs, there are several strategies you can employ to reduce your consumption. Simple things like accelerating and braking gently, avoiding unnecessary idling, and reducing the use of air conditioning can all improve your car's fuel efficiency. You could also consider switching to a more fuel-efficient vehicle or investing in an electric or hybrid car.

In conclusion, reducing transportation costs is a crucial aspect of managing household bills. By taking simple steps to reduce your fuel, maintenance, and insurance expenses for your vehicles, you could save significant amounts of money each year. Remember, every pound saved brings you one step closer to your financial goals and a more secure future for your family.

Do you feel like you're drowning in rent or mortgage payments? Are you tired of seeing your hard-earned money go to maintenance and insurance costs? Don't despair – there are ways to reduce these expenses and free up more money for your mental wellbeing.

One of the first steps to lower your housing expenses is to explore alternative options besides your current home. Have you considered downsizing or finding a cheaper rental? Are you eligible for any government subsidies or programs that can assist with mortgage payments? These options may take some research and effort, but they can be worth the savings in the long run.

Another method to reduce housing expenses is to negotiate with your landlord or mortgage lender. Can you request a lower interest rate or refinance your mortgage? Can you negotiate a lower rent or lease renewal price or offer to do minor repairs yourself in exchange for a lower rate? Don't be afraid to ask and present your case – you may be surprised at the results.

Finally, when it comes to maintenance and insurance costs, prevention is key. Regularly maintaining your home's appliances and systems can prevent more costly repairs down the line. Installing energy-efficient appliances and fixtures can also reduce energy bills in the long run. When it comes to insurance, shop around and compare rates from different providers to ensure you're getting the best deal for your needs.

By exploring these cost-cutting strategies, you can lower your housing expenses and free up more money for other important areas of your life. Remember, every little bit counts – so don't be afraid to make changes and explore your options.

Identifying and removing the expenses that do not align with our priorities and values is one of the key ways to cut costs and improve our financial stability. Many times, we may not even realise that we are spending money on things that don't matter to us. It's important to take a step back and evaluate our spending habits regularly.

To identify these expenses, it's helpful to create a budget and track our spending. We can categorise our expenses and see where our money is going. Then, we can ask ourselves if each expense is truly necessary or aligned with our values and priorities.

For example, if we're spending a lot of money on eating out, but we value healthy eating and quality time with our family, we can find alternatives like meal planning and cooking at home.

Another way to remove unnecessary expenses is to negotiate bills and services. We can call our service providers and ask for discounts or better deals. We can also shop around and compare prices to make sure we're getting the best value for our money.

By being intentional about our spending and removing expenses that don't align with our values and priorities, we can save money and improve our overall financial well-being. It's a simple yet powerful strategy that anyone can implement.

CHAPTER 4:

Revenue-Boosting Strategies

When it comes to generating more income, there are countless opportunities available to individuals who are willing to put in the effort. One of the most effective ways to earn extra money is by monetising your skills, hobbies, and passions through various channels.

For example, if you are a skilled writer, you might consider starting a freelance writing business or submitting articles to online publications for payment. If you are a talented designer, you could offer your services on websites such as Upwork or Fiverr, or create your own online design portfolio to attract clients. The key is to identify your strengths and find ways to market them effectively to potential customers.

Another approach to monetising your skills is to create digital products that can be sold online. E-books, courses, and tutorials are just a few examples of digital products that can generate passive income over time. By creating these products based on your expertise in a particular area, you can establish yourself as an authority in your niche and build a loyal customer base.

In addition to monetising your skills, it is also important to leverage your assets in order to generate more revenue. This might mean renting out a spare room in your home on Airbnb, selling items that you no longer need on eBay or Gumtree, Facebook, Shpock or Craigslist if based in the USA, or investing in rental properties or stocks with high dividend yields.

Finally, don't be afraid to think outside the box when it comes to building your revenue streams. Many people have found success creating and selling products on platforms such as Etsy or Amazon, launching a podcast or YouTube channel, or even starting a profitable blog.

Ultimately, the key to monetising your skills and assets is to remain open-minded and willing to take risks. With the right mindset and a bit of hard work, anyone can generate additional income streams that will help them achieve their financial goals.

One effective way to increase your income is by making money from your possessions, properties, and investments. This strategy involves identifying the valuable assets that you own and finding ways to monetise them. For instance, you could rent out a spare room or parking space in your property, sell unused items through online marketplaces, or lend out your money to others at an interest rate.

In addition, you could explore the world of investments and use your financial resources to generate passive income. This could involve buying shares in a company, investing in real estate, or putting your money into a diverse range of mutual funds or exchange-traded funds.

The key to making money from your possessions, properties, and investments is to identify the opportunities that align with your interests, skills, and values. When you find a profitable avenue, you should be prepared to put in the time and effort required to turn it into a sustainable income stream. By doing so, you can significantly increase your income and achieve your financial goals faster.

Reducing your debt burden and improving your credit score can seem like daunting tasks, but they can have a significant impact on your financial situation. With a lower debt load and a higher credit score, you can access better financial opportunities such as lower interest rates on loans, higher credit limits, and more favourable insurance rates.

One of the first steps in reducing your debt is to create a budget that allows you to live within your means while also ensuring that you are making all your debt payments on time. It's essential to prioritise your debts and pay off high-interest debt first. If you have multiple debts, consider debt consolidation to simplify your payments and potentially lower your interest rates.

Improving your credit score is another critical aspect of boosting your revenue streams. A low credit score can limit your ability to borrow money, rent an apartment, or even get a job. The good news is that there are some simple steps you can take to improve your credit score, such as paying your bills on time, keeping your credit card balances low, and monitoring your credit report regularly.

In addition to reducing your debt load and improving your credit score, there are other revenue-boosting strategies you can explore. For example, you could monetise your skills by freelancing or consulting, starting a side hustle or business, or renting out your property or possessions.

Ultimately, it's essential to remember that boosting your revenue streams requires effort, discipline, and a long-term perspective. By taking action and making smart financial decisions, you can achieve financial stability and freedom, providing a secure and prosperous future for you and your family.

Starting a business, freelancing, or consulting to create additional income streams can be a game-changing strategy in managing your household bills during a cost of living rise. Not only can it provide a source of extra income, but it can also offer you the flexibility and autonomy to pursue your passions and talents.

When it comes to starting a business, you have a world of options to explore. From e-commerce to social media marketing, to drop shipping and affiliate marketing, the internet has opened up a vast new world of opportunities for aspiring entrepreneurs.

By leveraging your skills and expertise, you can develop a unique and profitable niche that meets the needs of your target market.

No matter which revenue-boosting strategy you choose, it's important to recognise that there are potential risks and challenges involved. Starting a business or freelancing can be a daunting and time-consuming process, requiring significant investment of time and resources. Likewise, consulting requires a strong network of contacts and relationships, as well as a thorough understanding of your industry and area of expertise.

However, with the right mindset, skills, and strategies, starting a business, freelancing, or consulting can be a rewarding and enriching experience that not only supplements you're income, but also provides you with a sense of fulfilment and purpose. As you explore the various possibilities, be sure to stay focused on your goals, develop a solid plan, and seek out advice and support from trusted mentors and peers.

By adopting a comprehensive approach that combines cost-cutting, revenue-boosting, and saving strategies, you can achieve greater financial stability, security, and freedom for your household. As you implement these strategies and witness the positive results, you'll develop the skills, confidence, and resilience needed to navigate the ever-changing landscape of cost of living rises and household bills.

Any family or individual can benefit from the revenue-boosting strategies outlined in this book. One of the most effective ways to create additional income streams is by seeking the support of others. Friends, family, and peers can be excellent resources for advice, referrals, and partnerships.

Networking is a crucial aspect of any business and financial success, and it also applies to personal finances. You can network in various ways, such as attending events, joining communities, and engaging with people on social media.

However, the most effective way to network is by building strong relationships with people in your personal and professional circles. Your family and friends may know someone or have connections in the field you're interested in. They could help you make important introductions and referrals.

In addition to referrals, partnerships are another way to generate additional income. Collaborating with others who have complementary skills and expertise can lead to more significant opportunities and better results than working alone.

For example, if you're skilled in web development, but lack marketing skills, you could partner with someone who has those skills to create a more lucrative business. The same can be applied to any field or skill set.

Networking and building partnerships requires effort, time, and dedication. However, the potential reward can be worth it. By seeking advice, referrals, and partnerships you can increase your earning potential and achieve financial security and stability more quickly.

I will in my next book list ideas to help utilise your skills, passions, hobbies to earn an income.

CHAPTER 5:

Saving Strategies

Establishing an emergency fund is an essential aspect of personal finance management. It serves as a safety net for unforeseen circumstances such as job loss, medical emergencies, or unexpected expenses. In this age of rising living costs and economic uncertainty, having an emergency fund can be the difference between financial stability and chaos.

The first step in establishing an emergency fund is to determine its size. Financial experts recommend having at least three to six months' worth of living expenses in your emergency fund. However, the actual size of your emergency fund may vary based on your employment status, family size, and other factors. For instance, if you're self-employed, have a fluctuating income, or have dependents, you may need a bigger emergency fund.

The purpose of your emergency fund is to cover essential expenses during emergencies: rent or mortgage payments, utilities, food, transportation, and so on.

It's not meant to pay for discretionary expenses such as dining out, entertainment, or holidays.
Once you've established the size and purpose of your emergency fund, you need to choose a location to keep it. The ideal place for your emergency fund is a savings account that provides easy access to your funds while earning interest. However, it's essential to ensure that the savings account doesn't charge fees or penalties.

Automating your contributions to your emergency fund can be an effective way to build it over time. By automating your contributions, you ensure that a fixed amount is deposited into your emergency fund account every month without fail. This way, you're less likely to spend the money on non-essential items or forget to deposit it altogether.

In conclusion, establishing an emergency fund, determining its size and purpose, choosing an appropriate location, and automating your contributions can go a long way in safeguarding your financial future. A well-funded emergency fund not only provides peace of mind during challenging times but also gives you the freedom to pursue your long-term financial goals without worrying about unexpected setbacks.

One of the fundamental concepts that successful savers understand is the importance of setting specific, measurable, achievable, realistic, and time-bound goals. This practice not only helps them to create a clear plan for their finances, but it also motivates them to take action towards their goals.

When it comes to saving, the first step is to identify your purpose for saving. Do you want to build an emergency fund to protect yourself from unexpected expenses? Do you want to save for a down payment on a house? Do you want to save for your children's education? By defining your goals, you can determine how much money you need to save and how long it will take to achieve them.

Once you have established your goals, it is imperative to ensure they are SMART- specific, measurable, achievable, realistic, and time-bound. These criteria provide a framework that makes it easier to develop a clear action plan. Instead of setting a vague goal like "save more money," you can set a specific goal like "save £500 per month for the next 12 months to build an emergency fund."

It is easy to get disheartened when the intended results are not immediate, but when you create a timeline, you have something to work toward. SMART goals help to define precisely what needs to be achieved, by when, and how much you need to save. As you establish achievable milestones, you can track your progress and celebrate accomplishments.

In conclusion, establishing specific, measurable, achievable, realistic, and time-bound saving goals is crucial to reach the summit of financial success. By following this framework, you can stay focused on your end goal and stay motivated, ultimately taking one step closer to achieving your financial objectives.

As you embark on your journey towards financial success, a critical component to consider is selecting the right accounts, instruments, and portfolios that align with your personal preferences and goals. This decision has the potential to make a significant impact on your future financial wellbeing.

A crucial factor to consider when choosing the right accounts and investment options is your risk tolerance level. Your risk tolerance refers to the amount of risk you are willing to take on in your investments, depending on your age, income, and long-term financial goals. It's important to understand your risk tolerance because it directly impacts the types of investments you choose to make. For example, if you are a conservative investor who wants a guaranteed return, you may choose to invest in low-risk options such as bonds. On the other hand, if you are a more aggressive investor looking for high risk and potential high rewards, you may consider investing in stocks.

Another significant factor to consider when choosing the right accounts, instruments, and portfolios is your time horizon. Your time horizon refers to the length of time you plan to hold onto your investments. Typically, the longer your time horizon, the more risks you can take with your investments because you have more time to ride out market fluctuations.

Additionally, considering your personal preferences is vital when choosing investments portfolios. You must evaluate what you want from your investment before choosing any. What are you willing to trade-off between higher risk/higher reward?

To become successful while choosing the right accounts, instruments, and portfolios that suit your preferences and risk tolerance, you must gather as much information about the different investment options available. By educating yourself on this decision, this can go a long way in helping you achieve your financial goals while still being prepared for emergencies.

Managing your finances can be overwhelming, especially in the face of rising costs of living. However, taking action to manage your household bills and save money can be easier than you might expect. Building your emergency fund, saving for your goals, and investing for your future can all be achieved through a variety of techniques. One of the most effective ways to boost your savings is through smart budgeting.

Tracking your expenses and setting a budget that aligns with your financial goals can help you monitor your progress and make necessary adjustments. With so many budgeting tools and apps available, it's easier than ever to track you're spending and identify potential areas where you can cut costs. Automating your savings can also be a great way to build up your emergency fund or save for a specific goal. By setting up automatic transfers to your savings account, you can make saving a habit that requires little effort.

Another way to boost your savings is by reducing fees associated with your banking and investment accounts. By choosing accounts with low or no fees, you can save hundreds of pounds each year that can be put towards your savings goals. It's important to take the time to review your account statements and compare the fees associated with different financial institutions to make sure you're getting the best deal.

In conclusion, managing your household bills and saving money can be achieved through a variety of techniques, including smart budgeting, tracking, automating, and reducing fees. By taking action and implementing these strategies, you can build your emergency fund, save for your goals, and invest in your future with confidence. Remember, small changes can make a big difference when it comes to your finances.

As families seek to secure their financial future, it is crucial to diversify their investments. Diversification involves spreading your portfolio across various asset classes, regions, and sectors to minimise risks and optimise returns.

The concept of diversification is founded on the idea that different asset classes have varying levels of risk and return. While some classes have high potential returns, they also come with high risks. Others, like bonds and cash, are more stable, but the returns may be lower. By investing in different classes, you spread the risk across multiple areas, which reduces the overall risk of your portfolio. Regions and sectors are also essential factors in diversification. Economic and market conditions vary across regions, and the performance of companies in one sector may not directly affect those in another. Thus, investing in different industries and geographic locations can protect your portfolio from overall market fluctuations. Diversification requires careful research and analysis to ensure that different asset classes, sectors, and regions complement each other to achieve optimal returns. It is essential to strike a balance between risk and return, considering individual goals, risk tolerance, and investment time horizon.

By diversifying their investment portfolios, families can mitigate risk, optimise returns, and secure their financial future. Diversification, coupled with other saving strategies, such as creating an emergency fund, setting smart goals, and selecting the right savings and investment vehicles, sets the stage for financial stability, growth, and prosperity.

CHAPTER 6:

Monitoring and Adjusting Your Plan

As families and households strive to manage their bills effectively, it is important to choose the right metrics, tools, and frequency to monitor their finances. This allows them to track their progress and adjust their plans accordingly.

Firstly, families should identify the key financial metrics that are relevant and important to them. This could include tracking their bills-to-income ratio, monitoring their savings progress, or keeping a record of their debt reduction. By measuring and analysing these metrics, families can gain a better understanding of their financial health and where they stand in relation to their goals.

Secondly, families can use various tools and platforms to monitor their finances. This could include using budgeting apps, spreadsheets, or online banking platforms. These tools can help families visualise their financial data and make it easier to track their progress over time.

Finally, families should determine the frequency at which they will monitor their finances. Some may choose to monitor their finances on a weekly or monthly basis, while others may prefer a quarterly or annual review. The key is to find a frequency that works for their individual circumstances and allows them to stay on track towards their goals.

In conclusion, monitoring and adjusting one's financial plan is crucial to achieving long-term financial stability and success. By choosing the right metrics, tools, and frequency to monitor their finances, families can stay motivated and make the necessary changes to achieve their financial goals.

Assessing your achievements, challenges, and learnings is a crucial step to ensure that you are on track with your goals. Without regular assessment, it can be easy to lose sight of your progress and get discouraged. Therefore, it is essential to set up a monitoring system that allows you to review your financial situation regularly and identify opportunities for improvement.

One way to assess your achievements is to track your expenses against your budget. This will give you a clear picture of where your money is going and whether you are spending more or less than you planned. You can use budgeting apps, spreadsheets, or paper and pencil to keep track of your spending.

Another method is to review your debt reduction progress. Take a look at your outstanding balances and interest rates and see how much you have paid off so far. Celebrate your progress, no matter how small, and use it as motivation to keep going.
Challenges are inevitable, but they can also be opportunities for growth and learning. Take note of the obstacles you have faced and brainstorm ways to overcome them. It could be anything from an unexpected expense to a job loss or a decrease in income. By acknowledging the challenges, you can better prepare for them in the future and develop strategies to mitigate their impact.

Finally, it is crucial to reflect on the learnings from your financial journey. Take note of the strategies that have worked well for you and those that have not. Identify the skills and knowledge that you have acquired and think about how you can apply them to your future financial decisions.

Remember, assessing your achievements, challenges, and learnings is not a one-time task. It is an ongoing process that requires regular attention and adjustment. By staying aware of your progress and being open to making necessary changes, you can stay motivated and achieve your financial goals.
Identifying the potential risks, challenges, and setbacks that may affect your financial plan and developing strategies to mitigate them is an essential part of achieving your financial goals through cost management. While it's essential to have a well-defined plan and

roadmap to track your progress, it's equally important to be prepared for the unexpected.

In this chapter, we will explore some common risks, challenges, and setbacks that may derail your cost management efforts and suggest some strategies to mitigate them effectively. By anticipating and addressing these potential roadblocks, you can ensure that your plan stays on track and that you can achieve your goals.

One of the significant risks of cost management is underestimating the effort and resources required to achieve your targets. It's essential to set realistic goals and establish a feasible timeline that considers your current situation, lifestyle, and financial constraints. Try to break down your goals into smaller, manageable steps that you can accomplish gradually, instead of aiming for significant changes that may be unattainable.

In addition to that, emerging expenses such as urgent medical bills, car repairs, home damage, and other unforeseen events may threaten your financial security and compromise your cost-cutting strategies. To mitigate these risks, it's critical to have an emergency fund in place that you can rely on in times of need. Determine the size of your rainy-day fund based on your income, expenses, and other financial obligations, and regularly contribute to it until you reach your target.

Another challenge that you may face while implementing your cost management plan is resistance or lack of support from your family members. Achieving consensus and alignment on your financial goals and priorities is crucial to ensuring that your household works together towards a common objective. Involve your loved ones in the planning and decision-making process, and communicate the benefits of cost management in terms that resonate with them. Celebrate your wins together and encourage each other to stay committed to the plan.

Finally, external factors such as inflation, economic downturns, market fluctuations, or natural disasters may disrupt your financial plan and affect your savings, investments, or income. To prepare for these uncertainties, it's vital to diversify your financial portfolio, use hedging strategies to limit your exposure to risk, and stay informed about the latest market trends and news that may impact your finances.

In conclusion, identifying the potential risks, challenges, and setbacks that may affect your financial plan and developing strategies to mitigate them is a critical aspect of cost management. By anticipating and addressing these threats proactively, you can minimize their impact and stay on track towards your financial goals. Remember to review and adjust your plan regularly, stay flexible and adaptable, and seek professional advice and support when necessary.

Maintaining a positive attitude, celebrating milestones, and seeking support from accountability partners are important aspects of successful cost management. When we begin to implement changes in our spending habits, it can be easy to focus on what we are giving up rather than what we are gaining.

Additionally, seeking support from accountability partners can help us stay motivated and on track. Whether it's a spouse, friend, or financial advisor, having someone to provide encouragement and help hold us accountable can make a significant difference in our success. It's important to choose someone who is supportive and has our best interests in mind.

Finally, it's crucial to be flexible and willing to make necessary changes to our plan. Life is unpredictable, and unforeseen circumstances may arise that require adjustments to our financial goals and strategies. By staying mindful of our progress and open to making changes, we can continue to move towards greater financial stability and success.

Adapting your plan based on your changing circumstances, priorities, and market conditions is an essential part of successful cost management. While it's important to have a solid plan in place, it's equally crucial to be flexible and adjust it when necessary. This is especially true as circumstances beyond our control, such as economic turbulence, shifts in personal and professional priorities, or unexpected expenses, can significantly impact our financial situation.

To adapt your plan effectively, it's vital to keep track of your financial progress over time. This means regularly reviewing your bills, expenses, savings, and debts to see if you're on track to achieving your goals. You should also monitor your progress against specific milestones and timelines you've set for yourself, as this will help you identify any potential roadblocks or hurdles early on.

Another critical aspect of adapting your plan is anticipating and mitigating potential risks and challenges that may arise. For instance, if you're saving towards a goal that requires a certain amount of money, it's important to consider what you would do if unexpected expenses arise that might affect your ability to save. Similarly, if you're investing in different assets, you should keep an eye on market trends and make necessary adjustments to protect your portfolio.

Remember, adapting your plan does not mean changing your entire approach or strategy. Instead, it involves making minor tweaks and adjustments that align with your changing circumstances and priorities. For instance, if you've started a new job with a higher income, you may want to adjust your savings plan to reflect this change. Alternatively, if you encounter unforeseen expenses, you may need to allocate more funds towards paying these off, temporarily shifting your saving strategy.

Overall, effective cost management requires a willingness to adapt and adjust your plan based on your changing circumstances, priorities, and market conditions. This flexibility will not only help you stay on top of your finances, but it will also enable you to achieve your goals and maintain financial stability over the long term.

CHAPTER 7:

Conclusion

It is paramount for families to recognise the significance of managing their household bills effectively to attain financial stability, health, and happiness. Cost management is not only about saving money, but also about making mindful and conscious decisions to optimise household resources and align financial priorities with personal values. By adopting a proactive and deliberate approach towards managing bills, families can reduce their stress, enhance their quality of life, and achieve their financial goals.

Furthermore, cost management is not a one-time exercise, but a continuous process that requires ongoing attention, discipline, and creativity. Families should actively monitor their bills, income, and spending habits and make necessary adjustments to stay on track towards their financial objectives. They should also seek support from their network, including financial advisors, mentors, or peers, to share their experiences, learnings, and best practices.

The benefits of cost management are multifaceted and far-reaching. Not only does it improve families' financial health and well-being, but it also positively impacts their physical and mental health. By reducing stress, anxiety, and conflicts around money, families can enjoy better sleep, stronger relationships, and higher self-esteem.

Additionally, cost management enables families to pursue their passions, dreams, and aspirations, whether it is travelling, buying a house, or retiring comfortably.
In conclusion, cost management is a vital skill that every family should cultivate and master. It empowers families to take control of their finances, improve their standard of living, and realise their potential. By following the guidelines outlined in this book, families

can embark on a transformative journey towards financial freedom, health, and happiness.

Managing your financial situation can be a daunting task, especially if you have never delved into budgeting, saving, and investing before. However, the potential benefits and outcomes of applying the strategies in this book are numerous, and they can significantly improve your financial security and wellbeing.

By reducing unnecessary expenses and increasing your income streams, you can achieve your goals faster and with less stress. You can build an emergency fund that provides a safety net in case of unexpected events such as job loss, illness, or home repairs. You can save for your children's education, your dream vacation, or your retirement and enjoy peace of mind knowing that you are on track to achieve your goals.

Moreover, by diversifying your investments and adopting a long-term mindset, you can increase your wealth and generate passive income that supports your lifestyle and legacy. You can buy a property, start a business, invest in stocks, bonds, or mutual funds, and enjoy the benefits of compound interest and market growth.

However, the most significant benefit of managing your household bills is not financial, but emotional. By gaining control over your finances, you can reduce your stress levels, improve your relationships, and create a better future for yourself and your loved ones. You can focus on what truly matters in life, such as spending time with your family, pursuing your passion, or giving back to your community.

Therefore, I urge you to take action and apply the strategies in this book to your household bills. The road to financial success may not be easy, but it is worth every effort and sacrifice. Remember that you are not alone in this journey and that you can find support and inspiration from your family, friends, and networks. I believe in you and your ability to create a better life for yourself and those around you.

As families work towards implementing cost-cutting strategies into their daily lives, it is important to develop a clear plan of action to ensure the best chance of success. Setting actionable and measurable goals is crucial in any financial plan. These goals should be specific, realistic, and time-bound. Without a clear objective, it can be challenging to make progress or even know where to start.

Once goals have been established, it is important to prioritise them according to your values and needs. This will help you determine which areas you should focus on first as you work towards financial success. Consider trimming expenses in non-essential categories while looking for ways to increase income in others.
It is also important to commit to the plan and continuously monitor progress as you go along. Stay motivated by celebrating small victories and maintaining a positive attitude. Remember that managing household bills is a long-term journey, so be patient and stay the course.

Finally, utilise the resources and references outlined in this book to expand your financial literacy and further enhance your cost management skills. Commit to continuously learning and improving as you work towards financial stability, health, and happiness for your family.

A crucial aspect of managing household expenses is improving financial literacy. While this book provides comprehensive advice on cost-cutting, revenue-boosting, and saving strategies, it's important to keep improving your understanding of finance and money management. Fortunately, there are a plethora of resources available to help families explore and enhance their financial knowledge.

Websites (UK)

Websites such as Investopedia, The Balance, and NerdWallet provide valuable insights and advice on various financial topics, such as investing, credit management, and budgeting. Books such as "The Total Money Makeover" by Dave Ramsey, "Rich Dad Poor Dad" by Robert Kiyosaki, and "Money Master The Game" by Tony Robbins offer practical and motivational guidance on achieving financial freedom and wealth.

National Foundation for Credit Counselling (NFCC): NFCC is a nonprofit organization that provides financial counselling and education services. They offer guidance on credit, debt, budgeting, and housing. Visit their website at https://www.nfcc.org/.

Smart About Money: Smart About Money is a free online resource provided by the National Endowment for Financial Education (NEFE). It offers courses, articles, and tools to help individuals make informed financial decisions.

Explore their offerings at https://www.smartaboutmoney.org/.

Bankrate: Bankrate is a leading personal finance website that offers a wealth of information and resources. It provides articles, calculators, and tools on topics such as mortgages, credit cards, loans, and retirement planning. Visit their website at https://www.bankrate.com/.

Investopedia: Investopedia is a comprehensive resource for investing and financial education. It offers a wide range of articles, tutorials, and tools to help individuals learn about personal finance, investing strategies, and market trends. Access it at https://www.investopedia.com/.

The Balance: The Balance is a personal finance website that covers various aspects of money management. It provides articles and resources on budgeting, investing, taxes, insurance, and other financial topics. Explore their content at https://www.thebalance.com/.

Khan Academy: Khan Academy is an online learning platform that offers free courses on a wide range of subjects, including personal finance. They have interactive lessons on topics like budgeting, investing, and retirement planning. Find their personal finance courses at https://www.khanacademy.org/college-careers-more/personal-finance.

Remember to exercise caution and verify the credibility of any advice or services provided by these websites. It's always a good idea to consult with a qualified financial professional before making any significant financial decisions.

Foodbank Help & Advice USA

Feeding America: Feeding America is a nationwide network of food banks and food pantries. You can use their website to find local food banks near you by entering your zip code. Visit their website at https://www.feedingamerica.org/find-your-local-foodbank.

Food Pantries: Food Pantries is an online directory that helps you find food banks, soup kitchens, and other food assistance programs in your area. You can search by state, city, or zip code. Access their directory at https://www.foodpantries.org/.

211.org: 211.org is a helpline and online directory that connects people to various social services, including food assistance. By visiting their website and entering your location, you can find information on local food banks and other resources. Visit their website at https://www.211.org/.

AmpleHarvest.org: AmpleHarvest.org is a nonprofit organization that connects gardeners with food pantries to donate excess produce. They have a search tool on their website that allows you to find nearby food pantries accepting fresh produce. Access their website at https://ampleharvest.org/.

Salvation Army: The Salvation Army operates food banks and offers various assistance programs in many communities. Visit their website at https://www.salvationarmyusa.org/usn/ to locate your local branch and find out about their food assistance services.

Local Government and Community Websites: Check your local government websites or community resources directories. They often provide information on local food banks, food pantries, and community organisations that offer food assistance.

No Kid Hungry: No Kid Hungry is an organization dedicated to ending childhood hunger in America. They work to provide meals and support programs for children in need. Visit their website at https://www.nokidhungry.org/ to find resources, programs, and local partners that offer food assistance for children.

MyMoney.gov: This website is managed by the U.S. Department of the Treasury and provides a wide range of resources and tools for financial education. It covers topics like budgeting, saving, investing, and managing debt. Access it at https://www.mymoney.gov/.

When visiting these websites, you'll typically find contact

information such as phone numbers, email addresses, or online contact forms. Reach out to the food banks directly to inquire about their services and how you can access food assistance in your area.

Apps

Apps such as Mint, PocketGuard, and You Need A Budget (YNAB) can help families track their expenses, manage their budgets, and save money more efficiently. Other tools such as credit score monitoring services like Experian or Equifax or in the USA Credit Karma and Credit Sesame can help families stay on top of their credit status and improve their scores.

By using these resources and continuously improving their financial literacy, families can take better control of their household finances and feel more confident and empowered in their money management decisions. Remember, financial stability and success are not achieved overnight, but through consistent effort, education, and smart choices.

Mint: Mint is a free personal finance app that allows you to track your income, expenses, and budget. It provides insights into your spending habits, sends bill reminders, and offers personalised money-saving tips. Available for iOS and Android. Website: https://www.mint.com/

Personal Capital: Personal Capital is a comprehensive financial management app that helps you track your net worth, manage your investments, and plan for retirement. It offers tools for budgeting, expense tracking, and investment analysis. Available for iOS and Android. Website: https://www.personalcapital.com/

Acorns: Acorns is an app that helps you save and invest your spare change. It rounds up your purchases to the nearest dollar and invests the difference in a diversified portfolio. It also offers additional ways to invest and save money. Available for iOS and Android. Website:

https://www.acorns.com/

YNAB (You Need a Budget): YNAB is a popular budgeting app that helps you allocate your money, set financial goals, and track your progress. It emphasises the importance of assigning every dollar a job and provides insights into your spending patterns. Available for iOS and Android. Website: https://www.youneedabudget.com/

Digit: Digit is an app that analyses your spending patterns and automatically saves money for you. It calculates what you can afford to save and transfers small amounts to a separate savings account. It also offers a no-overdraft guarantee. Available for iOS and Android. Website: https://www.digit.co/

Honey: Honey is a browser extension that automatically finds and applies coupon codes when you shop online. It helps you save money by finding the best deals and discounts available. Available as a browser extension. Website: https://www.joinhoney.com/

Trim: Trim is an app that helps you save money on your bills. It analyses your recurring expenses and negotiates with service providers to lower your bills. It can also help you cancel unwanted subscriptions. Available for iOS and Android. Website: https://www.asktrim.com/

These apps can be valuable tools for managing your finances and saving money. However, it's always a good idea to review the terms, conditions, and fees associated with each app before using them.

Foodbank Help & Advice (UK)

The Trussell Trust: The Trussell Trust is a UK-wide network of food banks. They operate over 1,200 food bank centres across the country. You can use their website to find your nearest food bank by entering your postcode. Visit their website at https://www.trusselltrust.org/get-help/find-a-foodbank/.

Fareshare: Fareshare is a UK charity that redistributes surplus food to charities and community groups. They work with food banks and other organisations to provide food assistance. You can visit their website to search for local charities and projects near you that receive food from Fareshare. Visit their website at https://fareshare.org.uk/getting-food/.

Independent Food Aid Network (IFAN): IFAN is a network of independent food banks and food aid providers in the UK. They have a directory on their website where you can search for independent food banks by region. Access their directory at https://www.foodaidnetwork.org.uk/.

Salvation Army: The Salvation Army operates food banks and community centres across the UK. They provide food assistance and other support services. You can find your local Salvation Army centre and inquire about their food bank services on their website at https://www.salvationarmy.org.uk/.

Local Council Websites: Local council websites often provide information about food banks and other food assistance services in your area. You can search for your local council's website and look for sections related to welfare, community support, or food banks.

Citizens Advice: Citizens Advice is a UK charity that provides free advice on various issues, including accessing food banks and other sources of food assistance. You can visit their website at https://www.citizensadvice.org.uk/ to find information on food banks and local services in your area.

When visiting these websites, you'll typically find contact information such as phone numbers or email addresses. Reach out to the respective organisations or food banks directly to inquire about their services and how you can access food assistance in your specific location.

AFTERWORD

I am immensely grateful to the readers who have taken the time to read this book and have found value in its pages.

It is my hope that the strategies and insights shared in this book will help families manage their household bills more effectively, achieve their financial goals, and lead happier and more fulfilling lives.

Thank you all for sharing in this journey with me.